Vestry Book of
Elizabeth River Parish
1749 – 1761

Edited by
Alice Granbery Walter

CLEARFIELD

Printed for Clearfield Company by
Genealogical Publishing Company
Baltimore, Maryland
2011

ISBN 978-0-8063-5556-6

Made in the United States of America

Vestry Book of Elizabeth River parish

1749 — 1761

Edited

by

Alice Granbery Walter

1967

Permission for the publication of this Vestry Book
was granted by the Vestry of Saint Paul's Episcopal
Church, Norfolk, Virginia in a letter dated 24 Oct.
1968 and signed by Tazewell T. Hubard, Senior Warden.

Dedicated to the Memory of My Mother

ALICE HOGGARD GRANBERY

the Daughter of

MARY NASH (HERBERT) HOGGARD
and
HORATIO CORNICK HOGGARD

all

Late Communicants of Old St. Paul's

Her Nephew
Horatio Cornick Hoggard III
Was Elected to the Vestry
December 1968

PREFACE

The original of this Vestry Book of Elizabeth River Parish is in the custody of the Seaboard Citizens National Bank in Norfolk, Virginia. There are photostatic copies of it at the Virginia State Library in Richmond, Virginia and in the safe at Old Saint Paul's Church in Norfolk.

The editor has attempted to transcribe exactly the entire contents of the Vestry Book, and unless some unknown errors have been made there are no ommissions. The edges of some of the pages are torn or otherwise damaged, and some of the words are faded. In the case of illegible letters and words the Editor has inclosed her comments, or additions, in parentheses.

The two loose pages of Births and Deaths which are still existant in the original copy are indeed a lucky find. They are not included in the photostatic copies which were made of the book some years ago.

It has seemed unnecessary to include any history of the Church in this publication as that has already been published in the book "Saint Paul's Church 1832 - The Borough Church 1739" which was edited by Mrs. Calvert R. Dey, and published under the auspices of the Altar Guild of the Church in 1934.

Alice Granbery Walter

ACKNOWLEDGMENTS

The editor wishes to express her appreciation to the following persons who helped make this publication possible:

To Mr. Rogers D. Whichard for bringing the existance of this Vestry Book to my attention in his History of Lower Tidewater Virginia, and for sending his copies of the two loose sheets found in the original book.

To J. Hoge Tyler, III, President of the Seaboard Citizens National Bank, Norfolk, Virginia for the photographic copies of the two loose sheets.

To Mr. John W. Dudley, Assistant Archivist, Virginia State Library for furnishing the photostatic copies of the original Vestry Book, and for all of his courtesy and cooperation over a period of years.

TABLE OF CONTENTS

At a Vestry held Oct.r 1749

Present

The Reverend Mr. Charles Smith, Coll.o Geo. Newton,
Coll.o Will.m Crawford, Coll.o Sam.l Boush, Cap.t
Will.m Hodges, Cap.t Willis Wilson jun.r, Mr. Cha.
Sweney Cap.t Ja.s Ivy, Two Vestry Men being wanting
to supply the place of Mr. John Scott & Cap.t ___ Langly,
Tho.s the Gentlemen Present appointed Cap.t ___ Pheyp, &
Mr. Sam.a Boush to succeed them, who having accepted of
the Office; after having taken the Oaths enjoined them by
Law provided on Business; It. Upon ___ that appointed
Cap.t Willis Wilson & Cap.t John Pheyp Church Wardens
the former acting last year, & the latter in the room of ___
Cha.s Sweney he having declined who is ___ taken the Oath
of a Church Warden proceeded on Business, which was to
examine the Acc.ts against the Parish of Elizabeth River
which on examination is found to be Debtor to the particular
persons as follows

	Tob.o	lb.s
To the Reverend Mr. Cha.s Smith his Salary		16000
To D.o his salary for Preaching at Tanners Creek Chapple		__000
To Ja.s Prostear Clk of the Vestry		01000
To D.o Clk of the Parish Church		01000
To D.o Sexton of Y.o		00600
To D.o for washing the surplice		00050
To Mr. Tho.s Nash Clk of the great Bridge Chapple		01000
To Mr. Tanlys Estate 660 Mr. Tower 330 Clks of the Western Branch		00000
To Mr. Sam.a Tower Clk of Tanners Creek Chapple		01000
To Mr. Jn.o Hodges Sexton ___ of the great Bridge Chapple		00180
To Mr. Richard Edom D.o of the Western Branch Chapple		00200
To Mr. Wm. ___ for keeping the Western Branch Ferry		___00
To Cap.t Willis Wilson jun.r his Acc.t		00060
To Jn.o Colley for ministring & burying Ja.s Simmons		00__0
To Geo. Illsy his Acc.t		0__00
To Mrs. Barron her Acc.t		0____
To Doct.r Ramsay his Acc.o		0____
To Jon.a L. Tuna		0____
To Jn.o Donby for maintaing a child		____

X

<u>AT A VESTRY held 18 October 1749</u>

PRESENT:

The Reverend Mr Charles Smith; Coll^o Geo: Newton; Collo Willm Crafford; Collo Samuel Boush; Capt Willm Hodges; Capt Willis Wilson jun^r; M^r Ch^a: Sweny; Capt Ja^s: Ivy; Two Vestry men being wanting to supply the Place of Mr John Scott & Capt Saml: Langley Dec^d, the Gentlemen present appointed Capt Jno: Phripp & Mr Saml: Boush to succeed them, who having accepted of the Office, after having taken the Oaths enjoined them by Law proceeded on Business; the Assembly by Voat appointed Capt Willis Wilson & Capt John Phripp Church Wardens the former acting last year & the latter in the room of Mr Chas: Sweny, he having declin'd it who having taken the Oath of a Church Warden proceeded on Business, which was to examine the acct against the Parish of Elizabeth River which on examination is found to be Debt^r to the particular Parson as follows:

	Tobaco	lbs
To the Reverend Mr Chas: Smith his salary		16000
To D^o his salary for Preaching at Tanners Creek Chapple		04000
To Jas: Pasteur Clk of the Vestry		01000
To D^o Clk of the Parish Church		01000
To D^o Sexton of ....D^o		00600
To D^o for washing the surplice		00060
To Mr Thos: Nash Clk of the great Bridge Chapple		01000
To Mr Tenly's Estate 666 Mr Powers 334 Clks of the West'n Branch		01000
To Mr Saml: Power Clk of Tanners Creek Chapple		01000
To Mr Jno: Hodges Sexton of the great Bridge Chapple		00150
To Mr Richard Edem D^o of the Western Branch Chapple		00200
To Mr W^m: Baley for keeping the Western Branch Ferry		01500
To Capt Willis Wilson Jun: his Acct		00860
To Jno: Colley for maintaining & burying Jas: Simmons		00307
To Geo: Hoy his Acct		00100
To Mrs. Barron her acct		00200
To Doct^r: Ramsay his Acct		00500
To Dinah Dunn		01000
To Jno: Denby for maintaining a Child		00300

(corner of page is torn off)

Page 2 of Vestry Book

The Parish Acct brought over	D^t lbs Tobaco	31677
To Alex Collert for maintaining Hannah Hendrick		00150
To Sarah Millison a Poor Woman		01000
To Geo: Righton a Poor Man		00600
To Jno: Williams for keeping Bonedick Mason		00400
To Jno: Cooper for maintaining Kesiah Cooper		00200
To Jas: Tucker to maintain his Child		00500
To Thos: Watkins for keeping Edwd: Rolins		00700
To Martha Mason a Poor Woman		00500
To Henry Howett a Poor Man		00300

To Ann Howett a Poor Woman.....................................01200
To Jacob Cooper for keeping Geo: Cooper........................00225
To Law: Peede for maintaining Eliz: Sawyer.....................00600
To Susanna Cooper for keeping a Child..........................00534
(Total seems to be wrong?)   38939

To Jno: Grant for maintaining Mary Grant.......................00200
To D⁰ for maintaining Sarah Carter.............................00800
To Sam Cabowly? D⁰ Sarah Simmon to keep her next year..........00600
To Jnᵒ: Simmons D⁰ Thoˢ: Thynable to keep him near year........00550
To Mary Wood for keeping Thos: Dean 8 months @ 500 pʳ Annum....00334
To Marg: Hill for keeping Mary Hoblewaite?.....................01000
To Jno: Payton for D⁰ Ann Flannerkin...........................00150
To Sollᵒ: Moore a Poor Man.....................................00400
To Jnᵒ: Warrin a Poor Man......................................00800
To the Exoʳˢ of Edmᵈ: Anderson Decᵈ for keeping Blind Robin....00200
To Abraham Brice for keeping his daughter......................00600
To   Cooper a Poor Man..................................00500
To Mr Jno: Dupree as pʳ Acct...................................00882
To Mr Stephens as pʳ Acct......................................00228
To Mr Stroud as pʳ Acct..01830
To Mr Robᵗ: Waller his Acct....................................01900
To Willᵐ: Slatford...00160
To the Rev: Mr Chas: Smith his Acct............................02548
To Mrs Johnson her acct for maint: Mary Hudson, Princess Ann...06800
To Jas: Pasteur a Mistake last year............................00400
To Capt Willis Wilson his Acct for the N:West Bridge...........02000
To Mr Thos: Nash for Insolvents................................03162
To Jno: Grant for clothing Sarah Carter........................00200
To Edwd: Owens for keeping Ann Taylor..........................00600
To Tho: Collins for guarding the Prison........................00030
To Doctʳ Campbell's Acct.......................................0?888
To Wm: Hodges..00500
To Edmunᵈ Quin...02000
To Mrs Etheridge...00960
To Ann L ? 00500
   Tho: ? .... ?
Corners of this page torn off.................................

Page 3 of the Vestry Book

The Parish Acct brought over......................Dʳ.........67188
To 14 pʳcᵗ for collecting the Above Tobacco...................09405
                                                             76593

The Parish Debts for the foregoing Year amounting to 76593ˡ of Tobacco
being proportioned on 2337 Tytheables being the Number according to the
List this year returned amount to 33ˡ of Tobacco pʳ Pole.

Ordered that the Sheriff or Church Wardens collect of each Tythable
Person in this Parish the Quantity of 33ˡ of Tobacco & in case of Delay
or nonpayment to make Distress & Sail as the Law in that Case requires
& therewith discharge the Parish Debts.

2

Jn°: Hammon petitioned the Vestry for half the Parish Land which was allowed on his paying (38/1?) Annum his part not to interfere with the part whereon the House stands in where Wilder Lives.

The Hire of the Parish Negroes amounting to twenty three Pounds Six Shillings, Ordered that the Clerk collect the same & pay pt of the same to Mr Chas: Sweney his acct ....£ 14:18:11
& to Jas: Pasteur... 3:08:09
& the rest to be deposited in the Hands of Capt John Phripp, Church Warden.

(page 4 of Vestry Book)

AT A VESTRY held 9 October 1750

PRESENT

The Reverd: Mr. Charles Smith

Collo Geo: Newton   Mr Chas: Sweney
Collo William Craford   Capt Jn°: Phripp
Collo Saml Boush   Capt Willm: Hodges
Collo Robt Tucker   Capt James Ivy
                  Mr Saml: Boush junr

One Vestry Man wanting to supply the Place of Capt Willis Wilson Decd, The Gentlemen present appointed Capt Willm: Ivy to succeed him, who having accepted of the Office, after having taken the Oaths enjoyn'd him proceeded on Business. The Assembly by Vote appoint Capt Willm: Ivy & Mr Charles Sweney Church Wardens the former in the Room of Capt Willis Wilson Decd & the latter in the Room of Capt John Phripp having declined it. Who having taken the Oath of Church Warden proceeded on Business, which was to examine the Accts against Elizabeth River Parish which on Examination is found to be debter to the Particular Persons as follows.

To the Reverend Mr. Charles Smith his Salary   16000
To ditto his Salary for Preaching at Tanners Creek............... 4000
To James Pasteur Clark of the Vestry............................ 1000
To ditto Clark of the Parish Church............................ 1000
To ditto Sexton.....,...   600
To ditto for Washing the Surplice.............................   60
To Thomas Nash Clark of the Great Bridge Chapple.............. 1000
To John Hodges Sexton of the Great Bridge Chapple............   150
                                                              23810

To Samson Powers Clark of the Western Branch Chapple........... 1000
To Richard Edens Sexton of the Western Branch Chapple..........   200
To Sam: Powers Clk of Tanners Creek Chapple.................... 1000
To William Baley for keeping the Western Branch Ferry.......... 1500
To Mr John Dupree his Acct.....................................   832
To Thomas Nash for Washing the Surplice........................   60
To Capt John Phripp his acct.......................£ 44:18... 7184
To Capt Josiah Smith for Frances Thornton last year............ 1000

```
To Sarah Peaton for Frances Thornton............................1000
To Capt Pugh for House Rent to Condon.........£4.0.0............ 640
To Mr. Nash for Mr. Carringtons (Dissitteney?).................... 350
To John Drury for Maintaining Geo: Norah.......£4.13............... 744
                                                              39320
```

```
1750   The Parish of Elizabeth River                            Dr
       To Accos brought Over................................... 39320

9 October
To Doctor Archibald Campbell his Acco't .... £30.1.0 ............ 4808
To Eliza: Chilcutt for Mrs Smith for keeping her Mother)_
               £2.13.4 ......8 mos @ £4 pr annum   ) ....... 0426
To Mr Charles Sweny to make up the Money allowed for Building)_.. 2447
               Addition to Gt: Bridge Chapple £ 15.5.11 )  ··
To John Williams for maintaining Benedick Mason ................. 400
To Capt Hodges for Doctr Bundy's Acco........................... 800
To William Powel for keeping Mary Cottle........................ 300
To Capt Hodges Acco. £4.2.6  Tobacco /150...& 10................ 150
To John Warren a poor Man....................................... 1000
To John Seatton for Ann Flannerkin.............................. 500
To Ann Hewett a poor Woman...................................... 1500
To Henry Hewett for taking care of his Mother................... 300
To Margarett McNeile for keeping Hemsleys Child ................. 1500
To Mr. Strowd for keeping Susannah Johnson...................... 1000
To Johanna Haste keeping a poor Woman........................... 400
To Edwd: Owens for keeping Ann Taylor........................... 600
To Mrs. Barren her Acct........................................ 840
To Lam1: Calverly for Geo: Cooper 5.14.4 ...................... 914
To Elizabeth Thomas a Poor Woman ............................... 400
To Tho Low a Poor Man to be pd to Capt Hodges................... 500
To Jno: Grant for maintaining Sarah Carter...................... 800
To the Revd Mr. Charles Smith agt the Gleebe ................... 6558
To Jas: Pasteur his Acct....................................... 427
To Doct: Geo: Ramsey his Acct.................................. 2750
To Collo Moore a Poor Man...................................... 500
To Jno: Langley for keeping Sollo: Moor........................ 200
To Thomas Richardson for keeping Mary Richardson................ 180
To Jno: Hammond for his Acct. to be pd to Mr. Sweney........... 240
To Capt Jno: Phripp his fathur Acct............................ 228
To Susanna Cooper for keeping 2 children 9 mo:................. 750
To Do  for keeping Lam1: Wilson................................ 500
To Sarah Millison for keeping her Daughter...................... 500
To Mrs Furginson for keeping Betty Williamson 38/6 ............ 308
To Mary Fife for a child...... 3.0.8 ......................... 480
To Ann Barron for keeping Rose Mansfield....................... 192
To levy'd for walling in the Church Yard.......................25000
To Mr. Swiney for Clk & Sherifs Fees last year................. 9928
                                                              97817
```

4

The Parish of Elizabeth River (p 6 of Vestry Book)   D^r

To Acct brought forward...97817

To Mr Saml: Boush Junr................................. 120
To Capt Phripp his farthur Acct................................ 125
To Abraham Bruce for his Daughter............................. 600
To Ebinezer Stevins his Acct....... 1.14 272
To levy'd for building a work House for the Poor the
   Tobacco to be sold by the Church Wardens & Applyd to that use.20000
To Henry Pullin... 255
To Thos: Watkins for Rawlins.................................. 320
To the Estate of Edwd: Hensley........................... 608
To Lam^l: Calverly for Sarah Simmons...................... 500
                                                           120617
To 14 p^rc^t...............on the above Acc^{ts}.................. 16887
                                                           137504

The Parish Debts for the forgoing Year amounting to 137504 Pounds of
Tobacco being proportioned on 2500 Tythables being the Number accord-
ing to the List this Year returned amount to 55^{lbs}of Tobacco p^r Pole.

Ordered that the Church Wardens or whomsoever they shall depute collect of each Tythable Person in this Parish, the Quantity of 55lbs of
Tobacco, & in Case of Delay or nonpayment to make Distress & Sale as
the Law in that Case requires & therewith to discharge the Parish Debts

Ordered that Capt John Cook, Capt Jno: Phripp, Capt Max: Calvert & Mr
Chas: Sweny shall have leave & are hereby impowered to build a Gallery
in the Church in Norfolk Town, reaching from the Gallery of Mr. John
Taylor Dec^d to the School Boys Gallery equally betwixt them & their
Heirs forever to have & to hold

Ordered that Mr. Matt: Godfrey, Mr. Willm: Nash, Capt Trimagan Tatum &
Mr Willm: Ashley shall have Leave & are hereby impowered to build a
Gallery in the Church in Norfolk Town reaching from the Pulpitt to the
School Boys Gallery equally betwix them & their Heirs forever to have
& hold.

Ordered that Jas: Pasteur do have the Briks & Timber of the Old Church
to build an House on the School Land of Such Dimentions as shall be a-
greed upon betwixt he the said Jas: Pasteur & those who shall grant him
Liberty to build on the said Land.

                                                   Page 7 of Vestry Book

Ordered that the Church Wardens of Elizabeth River Parish do contract
with some Workman to build an House on the Parish Land according to the
following Demantions Vizt: 50 Foot long 20 Foot wide, with a Shade 10
Foot Wide length of the House; a Stack of Chimneys in the Middle that
shall make four Fire Places in it vizt: two in the fore Rooms & two in
the Shades. tilled Flours below & Plank above with a Shingle Roof Windows & Doors according to their Direct & that they put up the same to

the lowest Bidder.
Which accordingly was done & Joseph Mitchell undertook the same to fin-
ish as above for the Consideration of ₤131/10/00.

Mr Charles Sweny to the Parish of Eliz: River   D^r

To Cash Rec^d for the Hire of Davy...........................₤ 8/15/00
To D^o .... for Soll 6/10/00
To D^o .... for Ishmaell 1/10/00
To D^o .... for Sarah 1/10/00
To D^o .... for Nell 1/10/00
                                                            ₤ 19/15/00

Mem^r of the Negroes belonging to the Parish hired for the Year 1750

To Mr Andrew Sprowle, Davy ....₤ 8/15/00
To Mr Jno: Tucker, Soll: 6/10/00
To Jas: Pasteur, Ishmaell 2/00/00
                                                            ₤ 17/05/00

(1)   Ja: Pasteur Clothe
                  Vestry

PRESENT

The Rev^d Mr Charles Smith

Collo Geo: Newton   Capt Jno: Phripp
Collo Saml: Boush   Capt Jas: Ivy
Collo Will: Crafford   Capt Willm: Ivy
Mr Cha: Sweny   Mr Saml: Boush

The Vestry present by Voat elect Capt Willm: Ivy & Mr Saml: Boush
Church Wardens the former acting last year & the latter in the Room of
Collo Robt: Tucker having serv'd last year & declining it & after having taken the Oath enjoined them by Law proceeded on Business which
was to examine the Debts due from the Parish to the severall Creditors
which are as follows.

Tobacco

To the Rev^d Mr Chas: Smith his salary.......................... 16000
To his Salary for Tanners Creek 4000
To Jas: Pasteur Clk: of the Vestry 1000
To D^o Clk o'the Church 1000
To D^o Sexton & washing Surplice ....:   660
To Mr Thos: Nash Clk: o'the Great Bridge Chaple & Surplice...... 1060
                                                                ──────
                                                                 23720

To the Sexton .... D^o   150
To Sampson Powers Clk: o'the Western Branch Chaple 1000
To the Sexton .... D^o   200
To Willm: Balie for keeping the Western Branch Ferry 1500
To Mr Sweny's Acct ....ᶀ 5/13/4 for which he is allowed. 1000
To the Rev^d Mr Charles Smith's Acct ᶀ 3/18   624
To Mr Boyds Acct .... ᶀ 4/6   690
To Mr Jno: Willoughby's Acct .... ,'5/6   44
To Doct^r Campbells Acct p^r Agrm^t 20/0/0 3200
To Mr Dupree's Acct 4/11   728
To Mr Young for wrighting the Agreement between the)
Church Wardens & Mr Mitchell....................)   300
To Mr Saml: Boush his Acct 2362
To D^o his Acct Cash .... ᶀ 2/   320
To Richard Wood for keeping Thos: Deans 2 years 1200
To Thos: Hust's Acct ....ᶀ 5/3/5   828
To Willm: Ward for keeping Mary Wrighting   600
                                                                ──────
                                                                 58466

To Mary Wilder for keeping Lam^r: & Eliz: Wrightin.............. 1000
To Johanna Cooper for keeping Millison Wrighting...............   600
To Jno: Simmons for keeping Thos: Thylabale 2 years............ 1000
To Capt Willm: Ivy's Acct..........ᶀ /10/6   84

7

To Mrs Barrons Acct.. 5/......... 800
To Thos: Ward for keeping a Child 5 Months 500
To Jas: Deans for .... D⁰ 250
To Thos: Gordons for keeping a Child 5 Months 250
To Jno: Langly for keeping Sollo: Moore last year............... 240
To Jno: Grant for keeping Sarah Carter 3 Months................. 200
To D⁰ his acct for burying her 150
To Edmᵈ: Gwins Acct...................Ⱡ 1/10 240
To Elizabeth Cilcutt for keeping her Mother 800
To Capt Jno: Phripp Acct Ⱡ 12/11/3 2010
To Elizabeth Marnia 600
To Doctʳ Geo: Ramsey's Acct last Year 200
To Robt: Burgess his Acct ....Ⱡ /15/7½ 125
To the Widdow Powers for her Husband Decᵈ..................... 383
To Jas: Pasteur Clk: Tanners Creek 667
To Saml: Langley for Coffins 203
To Mr. Nash for a Tankard 40
To Sarah Peaton for keeping Frances Thornton 1000
To Capt Josiah Smith for Ann Lewin ..... Ⱡ 2/15/ 440
To Ann Barron her Acct 900
To Ebinezer Stevens Error last year 244
To Mr Saml Boush for Coppy List of Tythables 285
                                                              ‾‾‾‾‾‾‾
                                                              51627
To 14 pʳct ....on D⁰ 7260
                                                              ‾‾‾‾‾‾‾
                                                              58887

The Parish Debts for the foregoing Year amounting to 58887ˡᵇ of Tobacco
being proportioned on 2557 Tythables being the Number this year returned amount to 23ˡᵇ of Tobacco pʳ Ples.

Ordered that the Church Wardens or whomsoever they shall depute do col-
lect of each Tythable Person in this Parish the Quantity of 23ˡᵇ of
Tobacco & in Case of Delay on nonpayment to make stress & sale as the
Law in that Case requires & therewith to discharge the Parish Debts.

Ordered that the Collectors of Elizabeth River Parish for the year 1750
pay unto Capt Willm: Ivy & Mr Saml: Boush Church Wardens for the ensueing the 25,000 lb of Tobacco which was levy'd in the same year for the
walling in the Church Yard, which is to be by them appropriated for the
Repairs of the great Bridge Chaple & for maintaining the Poor House.

Ordered that Jno: Hammond & Jno: Wilder do move off the Parish Land by
the 25th of December next.

Recᵈ into the Vestry of Capt Geo: Whitwell Commander of his Majesties
Ship Triton a Silver Plate as a Compliment for his wife Mary Whitwell
being interr'd in the Churche.

The Vestry Hath agreed with Doctʳ Campbell to allow him 4000 lb of Tobacco for tending the Poor House as Doctor for this ensueing Year 1751.

                              James Pasteur Clk: the Vestry

ELIZABETH RIVER PARISH

The Vestry summoned & held this 16 December 1751 appointing Precessioners

PRESENT

The Rev'd Mr Charles Smith

Collo Saml: Boush   Capt Jam^s: Ivy
Collo Willm: Crafford   Capt Willm: Ivy
Mr Chas: Sweny   Mr Saml:Boush Junr
Collo Robt: Tucker

Pursuant to an Order of Norfolk County Court bearing date   November 1751
the Vestry of the said Parish mett and (torn) & appoint the severall persons to Procession in the several Precincts they are underneath command-
ed - Vizt:

SOUTHERN BRANCH PRECINCT

Mr Nathaniel Tatem and Peter Sparrow are hereby appointed to prossion the
Land from the Ferry Point to Etheridge Mill and that they make (torn) Returns of their Proceedings according to Law.

William Odean and Saml: Butt from Etheridge Mill to the great Bridge.

Joseph (ink blot) & Richard Jolliff from the great Bridge to Suggs M(ill)
& Edmonds Bridge.

John Murden & Benjamin Miller from Edmonds Bridge to hall-- poplar Swamp
& up pocoty Road to the Bridge the foreside Murden(s) Plantation.

Jno: Smith & Pelog Miller from the Bridge beyond Murden's by -- Field up
to pocety Swamp.

Nicholas Slack & Benjamin Butt from the hallow Poplar Swamp to the Norwest River as the County Bounds on the East side of the Road from the said
Poplar to the Norwest River.

Joseph Church & Maximillian Murden from the said Poplar to the Norwest
River the West side of the sd Main Road ----- Horn Quarter Road.

Jno: Prescott Junr: & Willm: Harden for the South Side of the Norwest Riv-
from the lowest Bounds of the County to the Cypress Branch.

John Taylor & Thos: Creekmor from the Cypress Branch up to the outmost
Bounds.

Lott Maund & Jno: Cherry, Son of Jno: Cherry from Suggs Millhead to new
Mill Creek.

Robert Burgess & James Ives from new Mill Creek to Batcheldors Mill.

Thos: Culpepper & Fos^t: Cherry from Batcheldors Mill to Taylor's Run & as far as usuall through the Gallberry Swamp.

John Wallace & Willm: Wallace from Taylors Run to the lower Bounds of the Southern Branch.

WESTERN BRANCH PRECINCT

Barneby Carny & Rich^d: Powell from Crany Island to Tait's Line.

Henery Creech & Enos Tait, from Tait's Line to Joliff's Line.

Jno: Joliff & Saml: King from Joliff's Line to Spring Line.

Ja^s: Jolliff & Matt^w: Sprivy from Spring's Line to John Tait's Line.

Willm: Bealy & Thos: Ellis from Tait's Line to Jonas Bruce's Line.

John Scott & Robert Culpepper from Jonas Bruce's Line to Jonas Taylors Line.

TANNERS CREEK PRECINCT

William Langley & Thelabald Junr from the land of William Langley's over to Prudence Williams to Sewells Point including all the Land on the North Side of Tanners Creek.

Thomas Talbutt & Jonathan Langley from the Land of Capt Tho: Willoughbys to the land of Danl: Godfrey.

Danl: Godfrey & Lam^l: Roberts from Danl: Godfrey's Land to Spratts Bridge & the land of the Widow Thelabald.

Joshua Nicholson & Willm: Ashley from the Land of the Widow Thelabald to Norfolk Town & to the Land of the Widow Morisson.

John Crutchet & Lam^l: Langley from the Widow Morisson's to the Mouth of Tanner's Creek, including all the South Side.

THE PROCESSION MASTERS HAVE ACCORDINGLY MADE THEIR RETURNS AS FOLLOWS VIZT:

BY ORDER OF A VESTRY HELD DECEMBER   1751

We the Subscribers have begun & presession'e all the Land from Coll^o Crafford's to the head of Julans Creek. We began at the Land of Coll^o Crafford in the Presence of George Veal & Thos: Edwards we p^o the Land of Mr Tucker and Thos: Harbort in the Presence of Thos: Brestin & Thos: Edward's. We por the Land of Capt Willm: Brestin & Thos: Edwards in the Presence of Capt Markom Harbort & Henery Habort. We por the Land of Henery Harbort and the Land of Markom Harbort and the Land of Edwd: Hughs in the Presence of George Veal & Thos: Bustin. We por the Land of Nathl:

Burgess & the Land of Jn⁰: Shaw & the Land of the Glebe in the Presence
of James Luellon & Thomas Collins we por the Land of William Porter &
the Land of Saml: Lewellin & the Land of Fra^s: Lewellin in the Presence
of Thos: Collins & Abram Meslor. We por the Land of Capt Jo^s; Smith &
the Land of Hel? Harbort & the Land of Ed^d: Davis in the Presence of
John Oans & in the Presence of Jn⁰: Lewellin. We por the Land of Gre
Dow & the Land of Jn⁰: Oans in the Presence of Wi^n: Porter & Willm:
Taylor. We por the Land of Jn⁰: Oans (Owens?) the Land of Thos: Oans
the Land of Wi^n: Oans the Land of Jean Taylor in the Presence of Edward
Taylor, William Porter, Jn⁰: Lewellin, Ed^d: Daivs.

> Jn⁰: Wallis
> Willm: Wallis

RETURNS made to by the processon Masters in Obedience of an Order of
Court held this 16 October we the Subscribers hereto by Virtue of the
Order have proceeded to procession all the Land in our Limitts.   1752

> John Smith
> Pelog Miller

IN OBEDIENCE to an Order of Vestry Bearing Date 16 December 1752 we the
Subscribers have mett & processond all the Land from John Jolliffs Land
to Jn⁰: Spring's Land Jn⁰: Jolliffs Line in the Presence of Ric^d: Bacon
& Willm: Bolton & Jn⁰: Ives? James King's Line Thos: Hopgood Capt Willm:
Hodges & John Taylor these four above mentioned procession'd in the pre-
sence of Aron Bolton, Willm: Wallis. Willm: Hopgood's Line & Coll⁰
Boush's Line Willm: Wallis Line Moses Richardson's Line Thos: Freman's
Line Jn⁰: Purkin's Line Jn⁰: Taylors' Line at the Beack Rige. Ja^s:
Talborts in the Presence of Ja^s: King, Ja^s: Jolliff, Ja^s; Hogges all in
peace & Quitness.

> James King
> John Jolliff

IN OBEDIENCE to an Order of Vestry Bearing Date 16 Dec 1751 We the Subscribers have procession'd all the Land from William Langleys & Prudence
Williams down to Coll⁰ Boush's.

Beginning first on the Line of the above sd William Langleys & Prudence
Williams, thence the Line of Mr Saml: Bartee & Zecariah Mason Bounding
on the Line of Mrs Eliz^t: Langley Relict to Mr Jo^s: Langley Dec^d thence
the Line between the sd Widow Langleys & Mr Jn⁰: Langley & Mr George
Langley, thence the Line between Mr Jn⁰: Langley & George Langley hence
the Line between Mr Ja^s: Thelaball Senr & Willm: Langley thence the Line
between Mr James Thelaball & James Thelaball Junr thence the Line Dividing or Bounding ____ Ja^s: Thelaball Junr & Mr Jn⁰: Langley & Capt Thos:
Willoughby & Mr Jonathan Langley the Line bounding Capt Thos: Willoughby
& Capt Ja^s: Ivy thence the line Bounding Capt Thos: Willoughby & Capt
Willm: Ivy & Willm: Tabbort thence the Line bounding Jn⁰: Tabbot ale
William Talbot thence bounding the sd Talbots & Mr Fra^n: Wishart thence
the Division Line of Coll⁰ Saml: Boush & the sd Mr Wishart & all the a-
forsd Lands & Lines prcession'd in the Presence of all the Proprietors

of the sd Lands as Within Mentioned. Given under our Hands this 17th
March 1752.

Willm: Langley
James Thelaball

MEMORANDOM of Land prcession'd p JOSEPH HODGES

My own Land present Sol^o: Savell & William Nicholson - Benjamin Hodges'
Land present Jeremiah Forman & James Hodges. W^m: Nicholson Land present
Benjamin Hodges & Solomon Savell, James Hodges' Land present Ben^n: Hodges
& Jeremiah Forman, W^m: Sikes's Land present James Hodges & Joel Sikes,
Solo^n: Savells Land present W^m: Sikes & W^m: Nicholson, John Germans Land
present W^m: Sikes, Joseph Curling & Solo^n: Savell, Jo^s: Curlings Land
present Jno: German & Pelog Mohoon, James Germans Land present Edwd:
Creekmor & Jo^s: Curling, Jer^h: Sikes Land present Jno: German & James
German, W^m: Hodges Land present

LAND Processioned p RICH^d: JOLLIFF

April ye 5th then prcession'd the Lands of Major Willis Wilson in Presence of himself & his son Thomas. Richard Joliff & Jno: Sikes.

Aprill 8 then precession'd the Lands of Jno: Ferebee, Jno: Grims & Ja^s:
Sikes in Presence of Ric^d: Jolliff, Edm^d: Creekmor, Alexander Forman,
Jno: Ferebee & Ja^s: Sikes April ye 11th then precession'd the Lands of
Mr Ja^s: Webb & the Lands of Ric^d: Jolliff in Presence of Ja^s: Webb,
Edm^d: Creekmor & Ric^d: Jolliff & the Lands of Jno: Skipwith, W^m: Hambsy,
Helery Hodges precession'd in the Presence of these four mentioned Persons.

IN OBEDIENCE to an order of the Vestry of Eliz: River Parish Bearing date
16 December 1751 directing the Subscribers to procession the Lands from
the head of new mill Creek to Batcheldors Mill have proceeded as followeth - Vizt:

The Lands of Francis Hewlit precessioned in Presence of Fra^n: Hewlitt &
Guils Randell the Land of Guils Randell precessioned in Presence of Guils
Randell & Jno: Williams the Land of Jno: Wallis precession'd in the Pre-
sence of Guils Randell & Jno: Williams the Land of Benjn: Bunting preces-
sion'd in Presence of Guils Randell & Jno: Williams the Land of Jno:
Williams Junr: procession'd in Presence of Jno: Williams & Willis Wilkins
The Land of Samuel Wilkins procession'd in Presence of Willis Wilkins &
Edm^d: Williams the Land of Jno: Williams Senr processioned in Presence
of Jno: Williams & Jno: Hewlitt the Land of Jno: Hewlitt procession'd in
Presence of Jno: Hewlitt & Rich^d: Hodges the Land of Thomas Fitzackly
procession'd in Presence of Jno: Hewlitt & Richard Hodges the Land of
Robert Burdgis procession'd in Presence of Jno:

(Note: This is the way the above ends. The previous pages, numbered
9, 10, 11, and this page **12** were numbered 42, 43, 44, 45, 46 and 47 in
the Vestry Book. They have been placed here for the sake of Cronology)

AT A VESTRY HELD Oct 23 1752

PRESENT

The Rev^d Mr Charles Smith

Collo Geor: Newton   Capt Jno: Phripp
Collo Willm: Crafford   Capt Ja^s: Ivy
Collo Saml: Boush   Capt Will: Ivy
Mr Char: Sweny   Mr Saml: Boush Junr
Maj: Willis Wilson   Capt Willi: Hodges
                      Mr Matt Godfrey

The Vestry present by Vote elect Capt Willm: Ivy & Capt Jno: Phripp
Church Wardens, the former acting last year & the latter in the room
of Mr Saml: Boush Junr & having served last year & declined it. And
after having taken the Oath enjoyned them by Law proceeded on Business
which was to examine the debts due from the Parish. Which was found
to be indebted to the particular Persons as followeth:

THE PARISH OF ELIZABETH RIVER D^r   Tobacco

To the Rev^d Mr Charles Smith his Salary   16000
To   D^o   for Tanners Creek   4000
To Ja^s: Pasteur Clerk of the Parish Church   1000
To D^o   D^o of Tanners Creek Chapple   1000
To D^o   D^o of the Vestry   1000
To D^o   Sexton of the Parish Church   600
To D^o   for washing the Surplice   60
Thos: Nash Clk o'the Southern Branch Chapple   1000
To D^o   washing the Surplice   60
To D^o   Sexton   D^o   200
To Samp: Powers Clk o'the Western Branch Chapple   1000
To Sexton   D^o   200
To William Baley for keeping ye Western Branch ferry   1500
To the Reverend Mr Charles Smith for Shrinkage of Sallery 800
To Mr John Deyerie? his Acc^t ₤ 3/3/6   508

Page 12 of Vestry Book

To Enos Tart for keeping Jno: Hobson omitted last y^r   700
To D^o as p Acc^t   116
To Coll^o George Newton as p Acc^t /8/8   64
To Willm: Ivy as p D^{le}   /16/   80
To Lam: Willoughby as p D^{le}   /33/2   267
To Thomas Newton as p D^{te} ₤ 6/18/4   1006
To Hugh Blackburn as p D^{te} ₤11/16/10   1898
To John Willoughby as   ₤ 3/19/11   645
To John Cann   ₤ 3/10/4½   565
To George Hayman   ₤25/ 9/1 3/4   4076
To Josiah Smith   ₤ 1/18/8   311
To John Phripp   5/00/0   800

13

To Wm: Young	3/10/0	560
To Ant: Lawson	2/05/0	374
To Eliz: Langley	42/00/0	6720
To Sam: Boush Jun:	15/19/6¼	2536
To Chas: Sweny	5/07/6	858
To Rev Chas: Smith	7/15/0	1240
To Dr Campell	17/13/6	3158
To James Pasteur	3/2/6	500
To Joseph Ellis	9/00/0	1443
To Arch^d: Campbell his annual Sallery		4000
To Patrick Murphy his wages for being overseer ₺ 10/9		2952
To Jno: Langley for keeping Sol^o: Moore omitted last y^r		920
To Tobacco levied to be paid the Church Wardens)_ toward maintaining the Poorshouse)		6000
To James Taylors Will to supply people with water)_ at the Southern Branch Chapple)		150
To Saml: Boush Jun: for a Parchm^t Book		400
To D^tr William Happer as p Acc^t for doctring sundry People in the Small Pox		1000
To Edw: Care for a Ththable overp^d last year		5/
To James Pasteur for procession Order & return		500
To Sam: Lamgley his Acc^t ₺ 2/3/6		412
		73536

Page 13 of Vestry Book

The Parish Debts for the foregoing Year amount to 83831 Pounds of Tobacco being proportion'd on 2439 Tithables being the Number this year returned amount to 34^lb Tobacco p Pole.

Ordered that the Sheriff do collect of each Tithable Person in this Parish of the Quantity of 34^lb of Tobacco & in case of Delay or nonpayment to Make distress of Sale as the Law in (that) Case requires & therewith Discharge the Parish Debts.

Ja^s Pasteur Clk o'the Vestry

Page 14 of Vestry Book

1753 October 20th - At a Vestry of Elizabeth River Parish were Present Coll^o George Newton, William Craford, ~~Robert Tucker~~, John Phripp, Samuel Boush Junior, Mathew Godfrey Junior, Charles Smith, Capt William Hodges, Capt William Ivy.

Mr. James Webb is ~~generally~~ Unanimously elected Vestryman in the room of Capt James Ivy deceased.

Math^w: Godfrey Junr Gent^n: is Elected a Vestryman of this Parish in the Room of Math^w: Godfrey Senr Gent who hath Resigned.

Math^w: Godfrey Junr Gent having been Elected a Vestryman of this Parish this Day took the Oaths to the Government And Subscribed the Test.

Resent Math^w: Godfrey Junr Gent^n

14

Willm: Ivy and Math^w: Godfrey Junr Gentlemen are Elected Church Wardens of this Parish for the Ensuing Year who having taken the Oaths of Church Wardens Entered into the Execution of their Office.

The Vestry haveing taken into Consideration the Several Claims Against this Parish Do Appoint As follows to wit:

Eliz^a: River Parish	D^r	Tobacco
To the Rev^d Mr Chas: Smith....................................	16000	
To D^o for Tanners Creek..................	4000	
To D^o four p Cent for Shrinkage........................	800	
To Ja^s: Pasteur Clk of the Parish Church 10 months..........	844	

Page 15 of Vestry Book   -   The Parish Debts brought forward   21644

To Ja^s: Pasteur Clk of Tanners Creek 7 months	594	
To D^o as Clerk of the Vestry......................	1000	
To D^o as Sexton	500	
To D^o for washing the Surplice	50	
To Geo: Chamberlaine proportion of Clk's Salary.............	412	
To Thos: Nash Clk of the Great Bridge Chappel	1000	3556
To D^o for washing the Surplice	60	
To Willm: Baily for keeping West^n: Branch Ferry	1500	
To Jno: Duprees Acc^t for Bread & wine	520	
To Thos: Mires for making Benches @ the West^n: Branch Chappel	620	
To the Rev^d Mr Chas: Smith his Acco^t	215	
To Sam: Power's Clk of the West^n: Branch Chappel	1000	3915
To the Sexton of D^o......................	200	
To Danl: McPherson for nursing an Infant 8 months	500	
To the Sexton of the Great Bridge Chaple.....	200	
To Mary White her Acc^t for the Fun^l: of Jno: Chatto........	140	
To Doct^r Jno: Ramsay for his Acco^t........................	2910	
To Geo: Chamberlaine for burying Jno: Chatto	45	3995
To Patrick Murphy	165	
To Lemuel Langley	80	
To Robert Waller	1104	
To Capt Jno: Phripp for his Acco^t..........................22100		
To Mary Marnix her Acco^t.................................	467	
To Phillis Colley her Acco^t..............................	84	24000
To Capt Josiah Smith for his Acco^t........................	500	
To Capt Willm: Ivy for his Acco^t.........................	1528	
To Rach^l: Oast for her husbands Serving 3 months Clk of		
Tanners Creek	250	
To Eliz^h: Chatto for Maintaining her Lame Child	1500	
To Barney Lorain for a Coffin for Lem^l: Boush	80	
To Saml: Langley for his Acco^t............................	230	4088
To Doct Arch^d: Campbell for his Acco^t.....................	1404	
To Geo: Bowin for Keeping Jesse & Keziah Manning two poor		
Children.................................	1200	
To Doct David Pursall for his Acco^t........................	516	
To Capt Edwd: Pugh for the Rent of a house	640	

To Mr Willm: Young for his Acco^t.......................... 120

Page 16 Vestry Book

Eliz^a: River Parish to Acco^t Brought forward.............   65078

To Mr Saml: Boush Junior................................. 2815
To Colo Robt: Tucker Acco^t Omited Last Year.............. 420
To Rich^d: Scott Acco^t D^o 154
To Mr Saml: Boush Junior................................. 1100   4489
                                                                    69567
                      4 p C^t for Cash................   2782
                                                                    72349
                  10 p C^t for Collecting.........   7234
                                                                    79583

By 2533 Tythables @ 32^{lb} p Pole...........................81056

By a Ball^e Due from ye Collector........................ 1473

Ordered that the Church Wardens do Collect of Each Tithable Person in
this Parish the Quantity of 32^{lb} of Tobacco And in Case of refusal or
nonpayment to Make Distress as the Law Directs.

                            Geo: Chamberlaine, Clk of ye Vestry

22 October 1754

Willm: Kitchin this day came into the Vestry and agreed to keep the
Poor House one Year from this Day for Sixteen Pounds for the Year.

AT A VESTRY held for Eliz^a: River Parish this 22^d day of Octr 1754

Page 18 of Vestry Book   PRESENT

The Rev^d Mr Chas: Smith

Col^o Wm: Crawford   Mr Saml: Boush Junr
Mr Chas: Sweny   Mr Math^w: Godfrey Junr
Capt W^m: Hodges   Capt W^m: Ivey
Col^o Geo: Newton

Mr James Webb being Elected Vestry man in the Room of Capt Jams Ivy Dec^d
and having taken the Oaths to the Government and Subscribed the Test also the Oath of a Vestry Man Enters on the Execution of his Office.

George Newton and W^m: Ivy Gent^n this day appointed Church Wardens and
they having taken the Oaths to the Government and Subscribed the Test
also the Oath of A Church warden, Enter on the Execution of their Office

The Vestry having taken into Consideration the Severall Claims against
this Parish do Appoint as follows:

Eliz^a: River Parish   Dr Tobacco

To the Rev^d Mr Chas: Smith 16000
To   D^o for Tanners Creek................. 4000
To   D^o four p C^t for Shrinkage 800
To Geo: Chamberlaine Clk of the Parish Church............... 1000
To D^o Clk of Tanners Creek 1000
To D^o Clk of the Vestry 1000
To D^o as Sexton and washing the Surplice..... 660
To Mr Thos: Morris for two years Service 800

                                                              25260

Page 19 of Vestry Book

To Tho: Nash Clk of the Great Bridge Chappel 1000
To D^o for washing the Surplice 60
To   Sexton of the Great Bridge Chappel............. 200
To Sam^p: Powers Clk of West^n: Branch Chappel.............. 1000
To Rich^d: Eadins Sexton of D^o............................ 200
To W^m: Baily for keeping the West^n: Branch Ferry........... 1500
To W^m: Portlock as p^r Acco^t............................ 316
To Mr Hugh McCoy as p^r Acco^t............................. 100   4376
To Mr Saml: Boush Junr as p^r Acco^t................... 429
To Mr John Dupree as p^r Acco^t........................... 600
To Col^o George Newton as p^r Acco^t..................... 133
To Capt Jno: Phripp as p^r Acco^t....................... 724
To Mr M   Meach for 9 months keeping ye Poor House ... 1920
To the Estate of W^m: Kitchen for D^o 3 months 640
To W^m: Sevill as p^r Acco^t............................. 250

```
To Doᵗʳ Jnᵒ: Ramsay as pʳ Accoᵗ.............................   2720  7416
To Capt Wᵐ: Ivy as pʳ Accoᵗ................................   1607
To Capt Wᵐ: Hodges as pʳ Accoᵗ.............................    292
To Docᵗ Archᵈ: Campbell as pʳ Accoᵗ........................    472
To Patrick Murphy for Samˡ: Pipers Accot...................    120
To Samˡ: Langley as pʳ Accoᵗ...............................    484
To Capt Wᵐ: Hodges for Richᵈ Eadins Accot.................    392
To The Revᵈ Chaˢ: Smith as pʳ Accoᵗ........................    500
To Hugh Purdie as pʳ Accoᵗ.................................    846  4713
To Dᵒ for keeping Lewis Connors 3 Childⁿ from the   )_ ......   2160
   6th of last Janʳʸ to this Day @ 6 pounds pʳ year)
To Richᵈ Harrison for his wifes Laying Sarah Welch.........     80
To Jnᵒ: Brown for Cloathing two Children of Jnᵒ: Tuckers....    300
To Geo: Bowin for Keeping Jesse and Keziah Mannin..........   1200
To Capt Josiah Smith as pʳ Accoᵗ...........................    860
To Jnᵒ: Wright for Keeping a Child of Danˡ: McNeals.........   240
To Joseph Weston as pʳ Accoᵗ...............................   1560
To Andʷ: McPherson for Keeping an Orphan of Jnᵒ: Jones......    880
To Jnᵒ: Wilder for Keeping an orphan of Phillis Browns......    400
To Capt Thoˢ: Newton as pʳ Accoᵗ...........................   1826  9506
                        Carrᵈ over                               51271
```

Page 20 of Vestry Book

```
To Mr Mathʷ: Godfrey Junr as pʳ Accoᵗ......................   6930
To Jane Stewart for Keeping her youngest Child ............   1000
To Mr Samˡ: Boush Junʳ as pʳ Accoᵗ.........................   1443
To Whitewashing the Bridge Chappel.........................   1000
To Docᵗ David Pursell as pʳ Accoᵗ..........................    602
To the Church Wardens for Publick Uses.....................    141
                                                              11116
                                                              62307
              To 14 pʳ Cent for Collection                     8733
                                                              71120

          By 2540 Tithables @ 28ˡᵇ Tobaᵒ p pole             71120
```

Ordered that the Church Wardens of this parish do Collect of Each Thithable the Quantity of 28ˡᵇ of Tobaᵒ and on their refusal or Non payment
to make distress as the Law Directs.

                    Geo: Chamberlaine   Clk Vestry

At a Vestry held for Elizabeth River Parish in the County of Norfolk this 21st day of October 1755.

PRESENT

The Revd Charles Smith

Colo George Newton	Capt Jno: Phrip
Colo Willm: Crawford	Mr Saml: Boush J^r
Capt Willm: Hodges	Mr Math^w: Godfrey
Capt Willm: Ivy	Mr James Webb

Elizabeth River Parish.....................................D^r lb Tob^o

To the Revd Chas: Smith his Sallery...........................	16000	
To D^o for officiating at Tanners Creek Chappel...............	4000	
To D^o four p^{ct} for shrinkage..................................	800	
To Geo: Chamberlaine Clk of the Mother Church.................	1000	
To D^o Clerk of Tanners Creek Chappel	1000	
To D^o Clerk of the Vestry......................................	1000	23800
To D^o as sexton and Washing the Surplice......................	660	
To Thos: Nash Clk of Great Bridge Chap: & wash^g Surplice......	1060	
To Mary Hodges for cleaning Great Bridge Chap^e...............	200	
To Willm: Grimes Clk Westen Branch Chapel Month..............	667	
To Rich^d: Edens Sexton of D^o..................................	200	3120
To Willm: Bailey for keeping Western Branch Ferry.............	1500	
To Thos: Morriss for his service at the Moth^r Church.........	400	
To D^o p^r Accot......................................	206	
To Capt Thos: Newton as p^r Account...........................	18045	
To Colo George Newton as p^r Accot.............................	1512	
To Mr James Holt as p^r Accot.................................	900	22563
To Capt Jno: Phripp as p^r Accot.............................	492	
To Mr Saml: Boush J^r as p^r Accot.............................	3430	
To Doct^r John Ramsay as pr Accot.............................	4012	
To Mr George Pool as p^r Accot.............................	396	
To Mr John Dupree as p^r Accot.............................	602	
To Mr Issac Moore as p Accot.............................	300	
To Capt Joshua Nicholson as p Accot.............................	466	
To Math^w: Godfrey as....... p Accot.............................	720	
To Phil deborn? for keeping Thos: Hard........................	300	10718

Page 22 of Vestry Book To Amount Brought over		60201

To John Wright for keeping an Orphan of Danl: M'Neil..........	1000	
To Geo: Bowen for keeping Jesse and Keziah Manning............	1500	
To Jno: Smith ....as p Accot......................	125	
To Capt Willm: Ivy.............as p Accot......................	480	
To D^o for Insolvents..........as p Accot......................	3384	
To Sarah Condall for keeping Geo: Crolls Child	336	6825

To Saml: Boush J^r as Bor^o: Clk 1b Tob^o 515)
To D^o as County Clk   520)-as p^r Acco^t 1035
To Moreck? Meach his sallery - Overseer of ye Poor House....... 2560
To Capt Willm: Ivy for keeping Ferry on Church)_
    Sundays since Last March....................) 300
To Mr James Webb as p^r Acco^t............................... 170
To Moreck Meach for his Wifes laying a Parish Negro............ 80
                                                              ————
                                                              4145
                                                             71171
                                                              ————
        4 p^c^{t} for Cash   2846
                                                             ————
                                                             74017
       10 p^c^{t} for Collecting   7401
                                                             ————
                                                             81418

By Mrs. Marg^t: Taylor for concealing five Tithables
to be paid by Mr Saml: Boush J^r 1250

By 2718 Tithables @ 29 lb ½ p pole   80181
                                                             ————
                                                             81431

Ordered that the Church Wardens or who Ever they deputed do collect for
each Tithable Person in this Parish the sume of twenty nine and a half
pounds of Tobacco and discharge the Parish debts: and in case of refua-
als or delay to make distress as the Law directs.

Saml: Foster by his wife came into Vestry and agreed to keep the Orphan
of Martha Hart dec^d one year from this day for 1000^l^{b} Tobacco.

Page 23 of Vestry Book   Octo^r ye 21st 1755

Solo: Sevil came into Vestry and Agreed to keep the Orphan of Eliz^a: West
dec^d one year from this day for 1000 lb Tob^o.

Mem^o: that John Wright who kept the Orphan of Danl: McNeil & George Bowin
who kept Jesse & Kezia Manning were informed by the Vestry that no farthur allowance should be given by them for keeping s^d Orphans.

Colo George Newton came into Vestry and prayed Leave to resign which is
granted and thereon Capt Thos: Newton was elected a Vestryman in the room
of Colo George Newton and he having taken the Oaths prescribed by Law and
subscribed the Test also the Oath of a Vestryman enters on the Execution
of his Office

Capt Thos: Newton & Mr Ja^s: Webb were this day chosen Church Wardens of
this Parish and having taken the Oaths &c.............................

Rich^d: Kelsick Esqr came into Vestry and paid Mr Ja^s: Bridges donation of
Ł 11/2/6
To Elizabeth Heay? for nursing & maintaining a lame Idiot last year Ł 6/0/0
To Abigail Watson towards supporting her four small Children Ł 4/19/4½
To Han: Page for nursing an Orphan of Martha Hurst dec^d Ł /3/1½
                                                           ————————————
                                                      Ł   11/2/6

At a Vestry Held for Elizabeth River Parish in the County of Norfolk this 26th day of October 1756

PRESENT

The Rev^d Mr Charles Smith

Mr Saml: Boush	Capt Thos: Newton
Mr Math^w: Godfrey	Capt John Phripp
Capt Willm: Ivy	Mr Ja^s; Webb

Elizabeth River Parish.. D^r lbs Tob^o

To the Revd Chas; Smith for his sallery........................... 16000
To D^o for officiating at Tanners Creek Chappel.................... 4000
To D^o four p^{ct} for shrinkage.. 800
To Geo: Chamberlaine Clerk of the Mother Church.................... 1000
To D^o as Clerk of Tanners Creek.................................... 1000
To D^o as Clerk of the Vestry...................................... 1000
To D^o as Sexton and washing the surplice......................... 660
To Thos: Nash Clerk of the Great Bridge Chappel................... 1000
To Mary Hodges for cleaning the Great Bridge D^o................... 200
To Thos: Granbury Clerk of Westⁿ; Branch Chappel................ 1000
To Rich^d: Edins Sexton of Westⁿ; Branch Chappel 200
To Thos: Morris for his service at ye Moth^r Church............. 400
To Colo Geo: Newton as p Acco^t.................................... 280
To John Dupree as p^r Acco^t..................................... 602
To Jno: Wright for keeping an Orphan of Danl: M'Neils   )
  & never to be allowed more hereafter for the s^d Child)-........ 700
  by Agreement   )
To Thos: Jones for Quit rents of the Glebe & poors Lands as p Acco^t 345
To Morach Meach for his sallery as Overseer of the poors House.... 2560
To Doc^t James Ramsay as p Acco^t................................ 4000
To Capt Jno: Tucker for his Acco^t Omited last year.............. 108
To Doc^t Arch^d: Campbell for D^o................................... 72
To Doc^t David Pursall for D^o.................................... 336
To Mr Saml: Boush J^r as p^r Acco^t.............................. 1082

Page 26 of Vestry Book   -   To Acco^t Brought forward............... 37345

To the Rev^d Mr Charles Smith as p Acco^t........................... 1145
To Capt Jno; Phripp as p Acco^t................................... 200
To Doc^t James Ramsay as p Acco^t................................. 1380
To Capt Thomas Newton as p^r Acco^t.............................. 17120
To Elizabeth Heage for maintaining her lame Idiot.................. 1440
To Mr James Webb as p Acco^t...................................... 52
To Mary Richards for keeping an Orphan of Jno; Hamiltons from
  ye 5th of Decr last to this day @ 1000^{lb} Tob^o p year........... 912
To Sol^o: Sevile for keeping an Orphan of Eliz^a; West
  Eleven Months at which time it Died.......................... 916

To Henry Stafford for keeping Eliz: Ward and agrees to)_ 300
   keep her of the Parish without furthar reward   )
To Capt Willm: Ivy as p his a^t for repairs ferrage & --- 351
To Willm: Wakefield for nurs9 & burying Edwd: Mariner 350
To Saml: Langley as p Acco^t...................................... 204
To James Wilson as p^r Acco^t...................................... 300
To Willm: Worminton for nursing & -- Hugh Fagan...................1200
To Edwd: Creekmore for dressing & ointment for D^o................ 440
To Willm: Bradley as p^r Acco^t................................... 320
                                                  63975

       To four p^ct for cash   2559
                                           66534

       To ten p^ct for collecting   6653
                                         73187

       C^r by A Ballance due from Collector   589
                                         73776

By 2784 Tithables @ 26^lb & ½ p pole   73776

It is Ordered that Capt Thos: Newton and Mr Ja^s: Webb be continued
Church Wardens for the Ensuing year and that the(y) collect for each
Thithable person in this Parish twenty six and a half pounds of Tobacco
and pay of the Parish debts with the same and in case of Delay or nonpayment to make Distress as the Law Directs.

Page 27 of Vestry Book   Octo^r ye 26 1756

This day Doct^r John Ramsay came into the Vestry and agreed to attend
and administer physick & ea to all the poor belonging to this Parish
within two miles of the Borough of Norfolk, and if he crosses the ferry
his ferriages to be paid for the sum of Twenty pounds p^r year to commence
from this day to be paid in Tobacco but in case he doth not chuse to take
Tob^o at such price as the Vestry shall rate the same at then the Twenty
pounds is to be paid him in cash.

                       Geo: Chamberlaine Clk Vestry

At a Vestry held for Elizabeth River Parish in the County of Norfolk this 17th day of December 1756

PRESENT

The Revd Mr Charles Smith

Colo Willm: Craford
Capt Jno: Phripp
Capt Thos: Newton
And

Capt Willm: Ivy
Mr Saml: Boush
Mr James Webb
Mr Mathw: Godfrey

Whereas the poors house belonging to this Parish hath lately been Burnt down by Accident

The Vestry present do Order
That another House be Built for the use of the Poor of the said Parish near the place where the other stood in manner and form as follows: to wit-
A Brick House thirty four feet long in the clear and Twenty Eight wide in the clear one brick and a half thick all the Partitions to be a nine Inch wall two windows in the front and two in the Back side the floor below to be tiled and the upper floor to be laid with plank a fireplace in each room at the Ends and to come out in.

The Bricks to be well burnt and the mortar to (be) made of three bushells of Lime to one of sand

And The Vestry then present do Levie the Following Quantity of Tobacco

Dr lbs Tobacco

Vizt: To Capt Thos: Newton towards building a house for the reception
         of the poor of this Parish in lieu of that lately burnt ,..... 9800
                          To four pCt for cash.....................- 392
                                                                    10192
                          To ten pCt for collecting...............1019
                                                                    11211
By 2784 Tithables @ 4lb Tobo p pole   11136
To a Ballance due the Collector   75
                                          11211

Ordered that the church wardens do collect for Each Tithable person in this Parish four pounds of Tobo and discharge the Above debt with the same and in case of refusal or delay of payment to make distress as the Law directs.

Geo: Chamberlaine   Clk Vestry

Page 30 of Vestry Book

At a Vestry held for Elizabeth River Parish in the County of Norfolk this 25th day of October 1757

PRESENT

The Revd Mr Chas: Smith

Capt Will: Ivy
Colo Robt: Tucker
Capt Jno: Phripp
And

Colo Willm: Crawford
Mr Saml: Boush
Capt Thos: Newton
Mr Mathw: Godfrey

The Vestry Having taken into consideration the several claims against this Parish do appoint as follows:

to wit

Eliza: River Parish... Dr lb Tobo

To the Revd Mr Charles Smith his sallery.......................16000
To Do for officiating at Tanners Creek Chappele............... 4000
To Do four pCt for shrinkage.................................. 800
To Geo: Chamberlaine Clk of ye Mother Church.................. 1000
To Do as Clk of Tanners Creek Chappel........................ 1000
To Do as Clk of ye Vestry.................................... 1000 23800
To Do as Sexton & for washing ye surplice.................... 660
To Thos: Morris for his service at ye Church................. 400
To Thos: Nash Clk of ye Southern Branch Chappel.............. 1000
To Do for washing ye surplice................................ 60
To Mary Hodges for cleaning Gt Bridge Chappel................ 200
To Thos: Granbury Clk of ye Westn: Branch Chappel............ 1000 3320
To Richd: Edins sexton of Ditto.............................. 200
To Morech Meach for being Overseer of ye Poor House.......... 2560
To Capt Thos: Newton Church Warden for his Accot.............33200
To Colo Geo: Newton as p Accot............................... 1239
To the Revd Chas: Smith as p Accot........................... 400
To Mr Samll: Boush Jr as p Accot............................. 1660
To Jno: Colley as p Accot.................................... 480
To Willm: Leonard as p Accot................................. 800
                                                            40539
Page 31 of Vestry Book -   Amt brot Over................... 67659

To Mary Richards for keeping Jno: Hamilton an Orphan last year 1000
To Thos: Jones for quit rents of ye Parish lands.............. 91
To Doctr Jno: Ramsay as p Accot.............................. 4731
To Saml: Langley as p Accot.................................. 160
To Majr Josiah Smith as p Accot.............................. 266 73907
To Capt Jno: Phripp as p Accot............................... 200
To Doctr David Pursall as p Accot............................ 200
To Capt Wm: Ivy for Cleaning Tanners Creek Chappel........... 100
To Henry Stafford for keepg Josha Wards 2 Childn 2 Mo........ 200
To David Maning for keepg Aron Barbers child 2 Mo............ 100

25

To Saml: Boush J^r as p Acco^t.................................... 280
To Arth^r: Turner as p Acco^t.................................... 130
To Thos: Nash for ferrages for ye Church services.............. 90
                                                                    1300

To Capt Thos: Newton to be sold and Applied to the support of)
    Mary Daughter of Eliz^a: Heag? in such manner & proportion)- 1200
    as he thinks fitt   )
To Levied towards bricking in the church Yard to be paid
    into the Hands of Thos: Newton 16000
                                                                   17200
                                                                   92407
                    To four p^{ct} for cash....................... 3696
                                                                   96103
                    To ten p^{ct} for collecting.................. 9610
                                                                  105713
By 2741 tithables @ 39^{lb} Tob^o p pole   106899
By a deposicturn due by ye Collector   1186
                                                      105713

Henry **Stafford** came into the Vestry and Agreed to keep Patience Ward from
this day to the next laying of ye Parish Levie for 500^{lb} Tob^o

Ordered

That the former Church Wardens be continued for ye Insueing year

And that they do collect for each tithable person in this Parish thirty
nine pounds of Tob^o and discharge the Abovesd debts with the same

Gio: Chamberlaing Clk. Vestry

At a Vestry held for Eliz^a: River Parish in the County of Norfolk the 24th day of Octo^r 1758

PRESENT

The Rev^d Mr Charles Smith

Colo Willm: Crawford   Capt Willm: Ivy
Mr Saml: Boush   Capt Willm: Hodges
Capt Thos: Newton   Mr Ja^s: Webb
And   Mr Matt^w: Godfrey

The Vestry having taken into consideration the severall claims against this Parish do Appoint as follows:

to wit

To the Rev^d Mr Chas: Smith for his sallery.................... 16000
To D^o for Officiating at Tanners Creek Chappel................. 4000
To D^o four p^{ct} for shrinkage...................................... 800
To Geo: Chamberlaine Clk of the Moth^r Church................... 1000
To D^o as Clk of Tanners Creek Chappel.......................... 1000
To D^o as Clk of the Vestry...................................... 1000
To D^o as Sexton & for washing the surplice................... 660
To Thos: Morris for his service at the Church.................. 400
To Thos: Nash Clk South^n Branch Chappel...................... 1000
To D^o for washing the surplice................................. 60
To Mary Hodges for cleaning South^n Branch Chappel............. 200
To Thos: Granbury Clk West^n: Branch Chappel.................. 1000
To Rich^d: Edins Sexton of D^o.................................. 200
To Morech Meach Overseer of the Poor House..................... 2560
To Doct^r Jno: Ramsay as p Acco^t............................. 3704
To Capt Willm: Ivy for cleaning the Chappele.................. 100
To Colo Geo: Newton as p Acco^t.................................. 122
To Hugh M'Coy as p Acco^t.. 220
To Capt Jno: Phripp as p Acco^t................................ 300
To Mr Saml: Langley as p Acco^t................................ 544
To Willm: Hodges J^r as p Acco^t.............................. 200
To Capt Thos: Newton as p Acco^t............................... 9046
To Mr Saml: Boush as p Acco^t.................................. 1571
To the Rev^d Mr Chas: Smith as p Acco^t...................... 380
To Henry Stafford for keep^g Patience Wards child 12 m^o........ 500
                                                                _____
                                                                46567
Page 33 of Vestry Book -   To amount brought over   46567

To Rachell Lewelling Wid^w of Thos: towards maintaining
   two Ediots......................£ 10.................. 1600
To Mr Ja^s: Webb ....as p Acco^t....................... 4194
To Sarah Ball for Nursing Aron Timberlake 12 M^o............... 640
To Nath: Fife? -- as p Acco^t.................................. 450
To David Bezill as p Acco^t......................£ 3 .
To Mary King for Nursing & ea Sarah Harris................. 200

27

To Benj: Hodges for Do Margt: Mollire 320
To Jas: Millerson for Buryg Wm: Millerson 100
To Jane Cooper towards Mantaining her 2 Childn............. 240
To Mary Richards for keeping Jno: Hamilton an Orphan....... 1000
To Geo: Chamberlaine as p Accot........................... 454
To Jas: Webb for Interest Allowed him for Expend: ₺ 26/4/4.. 160
To Levied towards Bricking in the Church Yards to)_........ 16000 25358
    be paid into the hands of the Church Wardens)
                                                                      71925

      Cr by a depositum from Collectr Deductd   1186
                                                            70739

      To 4 p Ct for cash   2829
                                                            73568

      To 10 p Ct for Collection   7356
                                         Total 80924

Cr 2907 Tithables at 28lb Tob is   81396
by a ballance due from ye Collector   472
                                     80924

Mr. Mathw: Godfrey and Mr James Webb are appointed Church Wardens for the
Ensuing Year and Accordingly took the Oaths of Church Wardens.

Ordered: That the Clk of the Vestry do publickly Advertisce that all persons who shall hereafter take any strouling Sick of indigent Person into
their houses without an Order or the concent of the Church Wardens or any
of the Vestry men for the time being shall at their own cost bear all dam-
ages that shall accrew by reason of having so taken them in.

Page 34 of Vestry Book   Octor ye 24th 1758

Resolved: That for the future it be a standing rule that all Orphan Children or such whose parents cannot maintain them and are above the Age of
four years shall be delivered to the Church Wardens in Order to be sent to
the Poor House -   Or that no Allowance shall be made by this Vestry for
keeping them unless it is done by Order of the Church Wardens or some of
the Vestry men.

This day Lydia Hamilton a Molatto bastard and Orphan of a White woman Nam-
ed Eliza: Hamilton was brought to the Vestry by David Bezill who refused
to keep the said Orphan to serve him Agreeable to the Act of Assembly in
that case made and provided. Whereupon George Chamberlaine Agreed to take
the sd Orphan to serve him agreeable to Law and to keep the Parish indem-
nified from any charge hereafter on Account of sd Orphan.

This day Mary Richards came into Vestry & agreed to keep Jno: Hamilton an
Orphan to the next laying of the Parish levie for 500 pounds of Tobo.

Ordered: That the Church Wardens or whoever they depute do collect for
Each Tithable person in this Parish 28 Pounds of Tobacco and pay of the
Parish debts with the same and in case of Refusall or Delay....&c......

                             Geo: Chamberlaine Clk Vestry

At a Vestry held for Eliza: River Parish in the County of Norfolk this thirtyth day of Octo^r 1759

PRESENT

The Rev^d Mr Chas: Smith

Colo W^m: Crawford   Mr Saml: Boush
Mr Chas: Sweny   Capt W^m: Ivy
Capt Jno: Phripp   Capt Thos: Newton
And   Mr Math^w: Godfrey

The Vestry having taken into consideration the severall Claims Against this Parish do Appoint as follows:

To Wit

To the Rev^d Mr Chas: Smith for his sallary...................... 16000
To D^o for Officiating at Tanners Creek............................ 4000
To D^o 4 p^{ct} for shrinkage.. 800
To Geo: Chamberlaine as Clk of the Mother Church 1000
To D^o as Clk Tanners Creek.. 1000
To D^o as Clk of the Vestry.. 1000
To D^o as sexton & for washing the surplice........................ 660
To Thos: Morris for his service at the church.................... 400
To Thos: Nash Clk of south^n Branch Chappel..................... 1000
To D^o for washing the surplice.................................... 60
To Mary Hodges for cleaning the South^n Branch Chappel........... 200
To Thos: Granbury Clk of ye Western Branch Chappel.............. 1000
To Colo W^m: Crawford as Adminis^r of Rich^d: Edins and   )
   to Thos: Bruce for the times they served to the W^{n}Branch)- ... 200
   Chappel as Sextons..)
To David Pursall............as p Acco^t........................... 385
To Robt: Waller............as p Acco^t......................... 450
To Capt W^m: Ivy ....as p Acco^t........................ 213
To Capt Jno: Phripp ....as p Acco^t........................ 180
To Thos: Jones............as p Acco^t.......................... 446
To the Rev^d Mr Chas: Smith..as p Acco^t..................... 492
To   to be by them sold and to)
pay Rachell Lewelling ₤ 10 for Maintaining her two helpless)-... 1500
   children the Overplus to be Accounted for   )
To Mary Richards for keeping Jno: Hamilton an Orphan............. 500
To Mr Saml: Boush..........as p Acco^t......................... 1441
To Abigal Connor for securing a drowned corps.................... 20
To Isaac Moor for summons a Jury of Inquest..................... 50
To Nathl: Fife for summons ? four D^o........................... 200
To Mr Ja^s: Webb............as p Acco^t......................... 1065
To Henry Stafford ....as p Acco^t.......................... 180
To Robt: Culpeper for the support of W^m: Colemans two children... 1000
To Capt John Tucker.........as p Acco^t.......................... 861
To George Chamberlaine......as p Acco^t.......................... 922
To Saml: Langley...........as p Acco^t......................... 180

To   be by them sold and to (pay))
       Thos: Newton ₺ 88/12/5 also to pay to Mathw:)-........ 18000
       Godfrey   ₺ 27/09/11 and Accot for ye Overplus) ....
To Doctr Jno: Ramsay for Attending the Poor & ea 4000
To Mr Saml: Boush towards bricking in the Church Yards)-.......... 12000
       but to be Accounted for to this Vestry   )
                                                              ‾‾‾‾‾‾‾
                                                               71305
                       To 4 p Ct for cash 2852
                                                              ‾‾‾‾‾‾‾
                                                               74157
                      To 10 p Ct for collecting 7415
                                                              ‾‾‾‾‾‾‾
                                                               81512
       Depositum in the Hand of ye Collector 1252
                                                              ‾‾‾‾‾‾‾
                                                               82824

By 2958 tithables @ 28lb Tobo pr pole 82824

The Vestry Agrees with Doctr John Ramsay that for the future he is not
Obliged to Administer Medicines to nor Attend any Sick but those at the
Poorhouse for the Sallery formerly Agreed on.

Ordered:
That Mr Saml: Boush receive the severall sums levyed towards Walling in
the Church Yards from the Collectors and put the same out to interest.

Ordered:
That Majr Jno: Willoughby and Capt Geo: Veale be invited to be Vestrymen
of this Parish, the former in place of Colo Saml: Boush Decd and the latter in place of Capt Willm: Hodges Decd.

Mr Mathw: Godfrey and Mr James Webb are continued Church Wardens for the
Ensueing Year.

AT A VESTRY HELD for Eliz^a: River Parish in the County of Norfolk this 20th Day of November 1759

PRESENT

The Rev^d Mr Chas: Smith

Col^o Will: Craford	Col^o Robt: Tucker
Mr Saml: Boush	Capt Jno: Phripp
Capt Willm: Ivy	Mr Math^w: Godfrey
And	Mr Ja^s: Webb

Maj^r: John Willoughby and Capt George Veale this day Attended the Vestry on the invitation of the 30th Ult^o and they having taken the Oaths of Vestry-men and subscribed the Test took their places Accordingly.

PRESENT

Maj^r Jno: Willoughby	Capt Geo: Veale

Eliz^a: River Parish	D^r	lb Tob^o

To the Acco^t for the several claims passed the 30th of Octo^r 1759 71305

To a Further sum towards Bricking in the Church Yards to be)
     paid to Mr Saml: Boush and to be by him Accounted for)-.... 32538
     the Next Vestry for laying the Parish Levy   )

	103843
To 4 p C^t for cash	4153
	107996
To 10 p C^t for Collecting	10799
	118795
C^r by 2958 tithables @ 40 p^r pole is	118320
To a Ballance due the Collector	475

Ordered: That the Church Wardens or whoever they depute do Collect for each tithable person in this Parish forty pounds of Tobacco and do pay of the Parish Debts with the same and in case the Delay Payment to make distress as the Law directs.

Ordered:
That Mr Robt: Tucker Junr be invited to be a Vestry-man of this Parish in place of Maj^r Willis Wilson who hath declined serving.

Page 38 of Vestry Book

Resolved:
That Mr Math^w: Godfrey and Mr Ja^s: Webb be continued Church Wardens for the ensueing Year. And they are hereby Impowered to let out the Building the Walls round the Church Yards to the lowest bidder at such time as they shall think proper.

31

Ordered
That the Clk of the Vestry do Advertise that the Building the Walls
round the Church Yards will be put up to the lowest bidder on the
        day of

The Vestry then proceeded to Appoint processioners as Recorded in the
Procession Book
                        Geo: Chamberlaine Clk Vestry

At a Vestry Held for Eliza: River Parish in the County of Norfolk this
17th day of Ocbr 1760

                        PRESENT

              The Revd Mr Charles Smith

Colo Robert Tucker   Mr Saml: Boush
Mr Chas: Sweny   Capt Wm: Ivy
Mr James Webb   Mr Mathw: Godfrey
Capt Thos: Newton   Colo John Willoughby
           and   Capt Jno: Phripp

The Vestry having taken into consideration the several claims Against
this Parish do Appoint as follows

To the Revd Mr Charles Smith for his salary............... 16000
To Do for Officiating at Tanners Creek..................... 4000
To Do four pr Ct for Shrinkage.............................   800
                                                                  20800

Page 39 of Vestry Book

To Ammount brot forward....................................   20800
To Geo: Chamberlaine Clk of the Mothr Church.............. 1000
To Do as Clk of Tanners Creek............................. 1000
To Do as Clk of the Vestry................................ 1000
To Do as sexton & for washing surplice....................   660
To Thos: Morris for his service at ye church..............   400
To the Clk of ye Suthn Branch Chappell & for washing Ye
    surplice.. 1060
To Do for cleaning ye Chappell............................   200
To the clk of the Western Branch Chappell................. 1000
To Josh: Bruce sexton of Do...............................   200
To the collector for a Ballance due to him last Vestry....   475

Nobr 17, 1760
To Jacob Wilder for summoning a Jury of Inquest...........   50
To Nathl: Fife for sumg Jurys of Inquest..................   400
To Capt Wm: Ivy as pr Accot...............................   110
To Mr Charles Sweny for his Acct to be brot in............   700
To Doctr Jno: Ramsay for his sallery...................... 4000
To Ann Posers for maintaining her 3 helples children...... 1000
To Ricd: Wm: Selvester for transporting Jno: Smith to
    ye poorhouse..   66

To Jno: Smith (ye Ditcher) a helpless poor man......... 300
To Wm: Moor for nursing Mark Flood.................... 125
To Abraham Bruce as pr Acct.......................... 61
To Saml: Langly as pr Acct.......................... 225
To the Revd Mr Charles Smith as pr Acct.............. 133
To Robt: Ives for a levy over charged last year........ 86
To Dotr Archd: Campbell as pr Acct.................... 420
To Mr Saml: Boush as pr Acct......................... 1697
To Capt Jno: Phripp as pr Acct....................... 165
To Geo: Chamberlaine Issuing procession orders) 1000
   and recording the returns   )
To Mr Saml: Boush for him to pay off all the cash Accts &
   the overplus if any to be accounted for the next Vestry

                        20000 37533
                             58333

To Dotr Jams Ramsay as pr Acct   Ꮀ 4/00/0
To Thos: Jones as pr Acct   0/14/4½
To Dotr Jno: Ramsay as pr Acct   1/01/6
To Mr James Webb as pr Acct   4/15/3
To Wm: Moor on Acct of Mark Flood   1/13/6
                     Ꮀ 12/04/7½

Page 40 of Vestry Book

To Rachell Lewelling for her maintaining her 2 helples children
                        Ꮀ 10/00/0
To Geo: Chamberlaine as pr Acct   3/07/9
To Mary Danahoe as pr Acct   1/05/0
To Capt Thos: Newton as pr Acct   92/08/5
To Mr Mathw: Godfrey as pr Acct   23/16/7
To the cash Accots brot Over   12/04/7½
                    Ꮀ143/02/4½

To the Tobacco Accots brot Over 58333
          To four p Ct for cash............ 2333
                              60666
          To ten p Ct for collecting   6066
                      1b Tobo 66732
          To a ballance due ye Collr   50
      By 3031 Tithables @ 22 p pole is 66682
                            66732

Ordered: That Joseph Mitchell have the Bricks --- of the Old Church
on condition that he clears the Church Yard of All the Rubish.

Ordered:
That Mr Mathw: Godfrey and Mr James Webb continue Church Wardens for
the Ensueing Year. And that they or whoever they depute do collect
for Each Tithable person in this Parish the Quantity of twenty-two
pounds of Tobacco and do pay of the Parish debts with the same. And
in case of delay of Payment to make distress as the Law Directs.

                      Geo: Chamberlaine Clk Vestry

At a Vestry Summoned & held for Eliza: River Parish this 20th day of April 1761

PRESENT   The Revd Mr Chas: Smith

Colo Robert Tucker   Mr Samuel Bush
Capt William Ivy   Capt John Phripp
Mr Thomas Newton   Mr Mathew Godfrey
Colo John Willoughby

Ordered that Robert Tucker Gent apply to John Randolph Esq Clerk of the house of Burgess for a Copy of the Law for Dividing the Parish of Eliza: River and that the said Robert Tucker Gent: Deliver the same to Benja: Waller Gent for his Opinion thereon to know whether the Poor belonging to the Other Parishes on the Division now at the Poor house in the Parish are not to be sent to the Respective Parishes and whether the Present Vestry should not meet before the time of Desolution to proportion the Expence of the parr Ministers Stipend and other Necessary Charges in the Inhabitants to be Collected at the time of the Collections by Law appointed on the whole as when the Parish was Int--?

                    Geo: Chamberlaine Clk Vestry

Here ends every Transaction of the Vestry of Elizabeth River parish till the said Vestry was dissolved, And the said Parish divided into three distinct Parishes as p Act of Assembly past April 6th 1761

Transferr'd to the new Vestry Book of Elizabeth River parish 1761

NORFOLK COUNTY

South^{rn} Branch acc^{nt} of ye Bearths of Ch taken senc ye 20 of October 1727

Maxemilion Murden son of Edward Murden born ye 21 Octo 17(27 torn)
1727 Alie daughter of Lem^{ll} & Bathiah Etheredge was born ye 15 Sept
Ann daughter of Joseph & Mary Miler was born ye 28 Septemb 1727
John son of Sam^{ll} & Mary S^{lade} was born ye 10 August 1727
Margrit Daughter of Philip & Ann Evens was born ye 14 Sept 1727
Elizth daughter of Edward & Mary Smith was born ye 15 April 1727
Elizth daughter W^m & Mary Overenton (Overton) was born ye 21 June 1726
John son of Joseph & Grace Warenton was born ye 15 January 172(7/8 torn)
Ann daughter of Mary Scofill was born ye 3 of February 17(27/8 torn)
Elizth daughter Thos & Sarah Whithurst was born ye 10 of Apr 17(27/8)
Dorcas daughter of Edward & Sarah Bright was born ye 27 of Fe(b 1727/8)
Alce daughter of Rob^{rt} & Alce Overenton was born ye 30 of June (1727)
Ledia daughter of John & Mary Ross was born ye 7 of Feby (1727/8)
Henry son of William & Dorothy Sikes was born ye 20 of June (1727)
Elizth daughter of William & Levina Ives was born ye 18 of April (1728)
Afiah daughter of W^m & Lizth Balentine was born ye 30 of Octo(ber 1727)
W^m son of Beniamine & Bathiah Cowel was born ye 27 of October (1727)
Bridget daughter of Richart & Dorcas Whitehurst was born ye 5 of Dece(1727)
Lem^{ll} son of Lem^{ll} & Sarah Wilkins was born ye 2 Decemb 1(727)
Matthew son of W^m & Sarah Etheredge was born ye 13 Decemb 1727
Mary daughter of Arran & Diana Sugg was born ye 19 December 1727
Lem^{ll} son of John & Sarah Hollis was born ye 12 of November 1727
Agnes daughter of Thos & Elizth Smith was born ye 7 of March 1727(/8)

Given under my hand this 18th of April 1728

Tho' Nash Ckofy Chap

(verso)
Mary Hebdon a Negro boy born ye 27 July 1727 name Sam

Acc^{nt} of Deths of people taken Senc ye 20 Octob 1727

.... wife of Cap^{tt} John Whidon Decd ye 31 of December 1727
.........ny daughter of John & Dorothy Creekmur Decd ye 4 of Jany 1727/8
..........n Stimson Decd ye 10 of January 1727/8
........p^{tt} Wm Nicholson Dec^d ye 28 of February 1727(/8)
Richard Nash Decd ye 14 of April 1728

To
        His Majesties Secretary's Office

Mary Dau^r of George & Dinah Collins born ye 28 Ap^r 1756.   Henry son of
Ditto born 23 Decem^r 1758.   John son of d^o born the 10 August 1760.

John son of Keziah Cooper born ye 29th Ap^r 1761
Jno son of Mary Coverly born ye 23^d March 1761
Eliz^h D^r of Mathias & Eliz Denby 15 March 1761
Jam^s son of Thom^s & Marg^t Marshall ye 2^d Ap^r 1761
Jonathⁿ son of Jacob & Sarah Wilder ye 8 Decem^r 1760
Robt Son of Peter & Marg^t Dise 29th Decem^r 1760
Eliz D^r of Jam^s and Ann Wilder ye 7th Decem^r 1760
Sarah Dau^r of Benjⁿ & Ruth Nabold ye 11th Decem^r 1760
Ake son of Rose a Negro Slave of Mathew Godfrey the 16th Decem^r 1760
Jemey Son of Rue a Negro Slave of Wilson Nickerson ye 9th May 1760
Moll Dau^r of Tamour a Neg S belonging to the Estate of Thom^s Husk decd.
           born the 10th April 1761
Pheby D^r of Nany a N. S. of James Thelobald ye 15 Sepr 1760
Jack son of Bridgett a Neg Slave of Ditto 25th Feby 1760
Hester Dau^r of Mary a N. S of Jno Griffins ye 6th July 1760
Bridgett Dau^r of Betty a N. S. of Lem^l Langley^s 26th Augt 1760. Dinah
           Dau^r of Grace a N. S. of Ditto 1st Novem^r 1760
Jemmy son of Hannah a N. S. of Jno Harberts 1 Septr 1755
Rose D^r of Ditto ye 9th June 1759
Moll D^r of Hester a N. S. of Geo. Abyvons June 9th 60
Kathⁿ Dau^r of Char^s & Ann Gore ye 30 March 61
Nancy Dau^r of Precilla a Molatta Slave of Jno Jone^s ye 12th Jan^{ry} 1761

(Editors Note: Please note that page 36 contains births and deaths of
the Southern Branch. This page 37 could be concerned with those persons
living in the Norfolk and Sewells Point area, but could also include
some Southern Branch families. John Herbert lived in the Southern Branch,
but Herberts also lived in the Borough of Norfolk.)

(Page 36 was damaged on its right-hand edge, and parts of the dates
are missing; those in brackets have been supplied by the Editor and are
believed to be correct. Fortunately, Thomas Nash dated his report mak-
ing it possible to judge the dates.)

INDEX

DUNN, Dinah 1
DUPREE, Mr. 7; Mr. Jno: 2,3,15,
17,19,21
EAGAN, Hugh 22
EDEM, Mr.Richard 1
EDENS/EADINS/EDINS, Richard 3,17,
18,19,21,25,27,29
EDMONDS Bridge 9²
EDWARDS, Thos: 10³
ELLIS, Joseph 14; Thos: 10
ETHEREDGE, Alie 37; Bathiah 37;
Lemll: 37; Matthew 37; Sarah
37; Wm: 37
ETHERIDGE Mill 9²; Mrs: 2
EVENS, Ann 37; Margrit 37; Philip
37
FEREBEE, Jno: 12²
FIFE, Mary 4; Nathl: 27,29,33
FITZACKLY, Thomas 12
FLANNERKIN, Ann 2,4
FLOOD, Mark 34²
FORMAN, Alexander 12; Jeremiah 12²
FOSTER, Saml: 20
FREMAN, Thos: 11
FURGINSON, Mrs. 4
GERMAN, John 12³
GODFREY, Danl: 10³; Mr. Matt: 5,
13,19²,27-29,30²,31²,33,34²,35,38
Mr. Mathew Jr. 14⁴,15,18; Mathew
Senr. 14
GORDON, Thos: 8
GORE, Ann 38; Chars: 38; Kathn: 38
GRANBURY, Thos: 21,25,27,29
GRANT, Jno: 2²,4,8; Mary 2
GRIFFEN, Jno: 38
GRIMES, Willm: 19
GRIMS, Jno: 12
GWIN, Edmd: 8
HAMBSY, Wm: 12
HAMILTON, Eliza: 28; Jno: 21,25,28²,
29; Lydia 28
HAMMON, Jno: 3; HAMMOND, Jno: 4,8
HAPPER, Dr. William 14
HABORT, Henery 10²
HARBERT, Jno: 38
HARBORT, Hel: 11; Capt. Markom 10²;
Thos: 10
HARD, Thos: 19
HARDEN, Willm: 9
HARRIS, Sarah 27
HARRISON, Richd: 18
HART, Martha 20

HASTE, Johanna 4
HAYMAN, George 13
HEAG, Mary 26
HEAGE, Elizabeth 20,21; Eliza: 26
HEBDON, Mary 37
HEMSLEY's Child 4
HENDRICK, Hannah 1
HENSLEY, Edwd: 5
HERBERT, (Harbort) Henery 10²;
(Harbort) Hel: 11; (Harbort)
John 38²; (Harbort) Capt.
Markom 10²; Thos: 10
HEWETT, Ann 4; Henry 4
HEWLIT/HEWLITT, Francis 12²;
Jno: 12⁴
HILL, Marg: 2
HOBLEWAITE, Mary 2
HODGES, Benn: 12; Benjamin 12²;
Benj: 28; Capt. 4³; Helery 12;
(Hogges) Jas: 11; James 12⁴;
Mr. Jno: 1,3; Joseph 12; Mary
19,21,25,27,29; Richd: 12²;
Capt. Willm: 1,3,11,13,14,17,
18²,19,27, decd 30; Willm: Jr.
27; Wm: 2,12
HOGGES, Jas: 11
HOLLIS, John 37; Lemll: 37;
Sarah 37
HOLT, Mr. James 19
HOPGOOD, Thos: 11; Willm: 11
HOWETT, Ann 2; Henry 1
HOY, George 1
HUDSON, Mary 2
HUGHS, Edwd: 10
HURST, Martha 20
HUSK decd, Thoms: 38
HUST, Thos: 7
IVES, Elizth: 37; James 9; Capt.
James decd. 17; Jno: 11; Levina
37; Robt: 34; William 37
IVEY/IVY, Capt. James 1,3,7,9,11,
12,14; Capt. William/Willm:/Wm:
3²,7³,8,9,11,13²,14,15,17²,18,
19²,20-23,25²,27²,29², 31,33²,35
JOHNSON, Mrs. 2; Susannah 4
JOLIF/JOLLIF/JOLLIFF, Jas: 10,11;
Jno: 10,11²,Richard 9,12⁵
JONES, Jno: 18,38; Thos: 21,25,29,
34
KELSICK, Richd: 20
KING, James 11²; Mary 27; Saml: 10
KITCHIN, Willm: 16; Wm: 17

L------ , Ann 2
LANGLEY/LANGLY, Mrs. Elizt: relict
  11; Eliz: 14; Mr. George 11[2];
  Jno: 4,8,11[3],14; Jonathan 10,11;
  Mr. Jos: decd. 11; Laml: 10;
  Lemuel 15,38; Capt. Saml: 1,8,
  14.15,18,22,25,27,29,34; widow
  11; William/Willm: 10[2],11[3],12
LAWSON, Ant: 14
LEONARD Willm: 25
LEWELLIN/LEWELLING/LUELLON, Fras:
  11; James 11; Jno: 11[2]; Rachell
  27,29,34; Saml: 11; Thos: 27
LEWIN, Ann 8
LORAIN, Barney 15
LOW, He: 4
MANING, David 25
MANNIN/MANNING, Jesse 15,18,19,20
  Keziah 15,18,19,20
MANSFIELD, Rose 4
MARINER, Edwd: 22
MARNIA, Elizabeth 8
MANIX, Mary 15
MARSHALL, Jams: 38; Margt: 38;
  Thoms: 38
MASON/MESON, Bonedick 1; Benedick
  4; Martha 1, Zecariah 11
MAUND, Lott 9
McCOY, Mr. Hugh 17,27
McNeal, Danl: 18; orphan of 19-21
McNEILE, Margarett 4
McPHERSON, Andw: 18; Danl: 15
MEACH, Mr. M-----17; Moreck 20[2];
  Morach 21; Morech 25,27
MESLOR, Abram 11
MILER, Ann 37; Joseph 37; Mary 37
MILLER, Benjamin 9; Pelog 9,11
MILLERSON, Jas: 28; Wm: 28
MILLISON, Sarah 1,4
MIRES, Thos: 15
MITCHELL, Mr. 7; Joseph 6,34
MOHOON, Peleg 12
MOLLIRE, Margt: 28
MOOR/MOORE, Collo: 4; Mr. Isaac
  19,29; Sollo: 2,4,8,14; Wm: 34[2]
MORISSON, widow 10[2]
MORRIS, Mr. Thos: 17,19,21,25,27,
  29,33
MURDEN, Edward 37; John 9; Maxe-
  milion 37; Maximillion 9
MURPHY, Patrick 14,15,18
NABOLD, Benjn:, Ruth, Sarah 38

NASH, Mr. 4,8; Richard 37; Mr.
  Thomas 1,2,3[2],7,13,15,17,19,21,
  25-27,29,37,38; Mr. Willm: 5
NEWTON, Collo: Geo: 1,3,7,13[2],14,
  17[3],19[2],20[2],21[2],22,23[2],25[2],26[2],
  27[2],29,33,34; Thomas 13,30,35
NICHOLSON, Joshua 10; Capt. Joshua
  19; William 12[3]; --ptt: Wm: 37
NICKERSON, Wilson 38
NORAH, Geo: 4
OANS, John 11[2]; Thos: 11; Wm: 11
OAST, Rachl: 15
ODEAN, William 9
OVERENTON (Overton?), Alce 37[2];
  Elizth: 37; Mary 37; Robt: 37;
  Wm: 37
OWENS (see OANS), Edwd: 2,4
PAGE, Han: 20
PASTEUR, Jas: 1,2,3[2],4,5[2],6,7,8[2],
  13,14[3],15[2]
PAYTON, Sarah 4,8
PEEDE, Law: 2
PHRIPP, Capt. 5; Capt Jno:/John
  1[2], 3[4], 4, 5[2],7,8,13[3],14,15,17,
  19[2],21[2],22,25[2],27,29[2],31,33-35
PIPER, Saml: 18
POOL, Mr. George 19
PORTER, William 11[2]
PORTLOCK, Wm: 17
POSERS, Ann 33
POWEL, William 4; Richd: 10
POWERS, Mr. 1; Sam: 3 15; Mr. Saml:
  1,3; Samp: 13,17; Sampson 3,7;
  widow 8
PRESCOTT, Jno: Jr. 9
PUGH, Capt. 4; Capt. Edwd: 15
PULLIN, Henry 5
PURDIE, Hugh 18
PURKINS, Jno: 11
PURSALL/PURSELL, Dr. David 15,18[2],
  21,25,29
QUIN, Edmund 2
RAMSAY/RAMSEY, Dr. 1; Dr. Geo: 4;
  Dr. James 21[2],34; Dr. Jno: 15,
  18,19,22,25,27,30[2],33,34
RANDALL, Guils: 12[5]
RANDOLPH, esq, John 35
RAWLINS, ---- 5
RICHARDS, Mary 21,25,28[2],29
RICHARDSON, Mary 4; Moses 11; Tho-
  mas 4
RIGHTON, Geo: 1

ROBERTS, Laml: 10
ROBIN, Blind 2
ROBINS, Edwd: 1
ROSS, John 37; Ledia 37; Mary 37
SAVELL, Solo: 12[3] (see Sevil)
SAWYER, Eliz: 2
SCOFILL, Ann 37; Mary 37
SCOTT, Mr. John 1,10; Richd: 16
SEATON, John 4
SELVESTER, Richd: Wm: 33
SEVIL/SEVILE (see SAVELL)
  Solo: 20,21[2]; Wm: 17
SHAW, Jno: 11
SIKES, Dorothy 37; Henry 37; Jas:
  12[2]; Jerh: 12; Joel 12; Jno: 12;
  William 12[3],37
SIMMONS, Jas: 1; Jno: 2,7; Sarah
  2,5
SKIPWITH, Jno: 12
SLACK, Nicholas 9
SLADE, John 37; Mary 37; Samll:37
SLATFORD, Willm: 2
SLAVES, 6,38
SMITH, Agnes 37, Revd. Mr. Charles
  1[2],2,3[2],4,7[3],9,13[3],14[2],15[2],17[2],
  18,19[2],21[2],23,25[3],27[3],29[3],31,33[2],
  34,35; Edward 37; Elizth: 37[2];
  Jno: 9,19,33,34; John 11; Capt.
  Jos: 11; Josiah 13; Capt. Josiah
  3,8,15,18 Majr. Josiah 25; Mary
  37; Mrs. 4; Thos: 37
SPARROW, Peter 9
SPRING, 10[2], Jno: 11
SPRIVY (Spivey?), Mattw: 10
SPROWLE, Mr. Andrew 6
STAFFORD, Henry 22,25,26,27,29
STEPHENS, Mr. 2
STEVENS/STEVINS, Ebinezer 5,8
STEWART, Jane 18
STIMSON, ----n 37
STROUD/STROWD, Mr. 2,4
SUGG, 9; Arran 37; Diana 37; Mary
  37
SWENEY/SWENY/SWINEY, Mr. 4,7;
  Mr. Chas: 1[2],3[3],4-7,9,12,14,17,
  29,33[2]
TABBORT (Talbot?), Willm: 11
TABBOT, Jno: 11
TAIT, Enos 10; John 10
TALBORTS, Jas: 11
TALBOT, Jno: 11; Wm: 11[2]
TALBUTT, Thomas 10

TART, Enos 13
TATEM/TATUM, Mr. Nathaniel 9;
  Capt. Trimagan 5
TAYLOR, Ann 2,4; Edward 11;
  James 14; Jean 11; Mr. John 5;
  John 9, 11; Margt: 20
TENLEY, Estate of Mr. 1
THELABALL/THELOBALL, (see
  Thylabale & Thynable) James
  12,38; -- Jr 10; Mr. James
  Jr. 11[2]; Mr. James Senr. 11[2];
  (Thylabale) Thos: 7; (Thynable)
  Thos: 2; widow 10[2]
THOMAS, Elizabeth 4
THORNTON, Frances 3,4,8
THYLABALE, Thos: 7
THYNABLE, Thos: 2
TIMBERLAKE, Aron 27
TUCKER, Jas: 1; Mr. Jno: 6,18;
  Capt. Jno: 21,29; Mr. 10: Collo.
  Robt: 3,7,9,14,16,25,31,33,35[3];
  Mr. Robt: Jr. 31
TURNER, Arthur 26
VEAL, George 10[2]; Capt. Geo: 30,
  31[2]
WAKEFIELD, Willm: 22
WALLACE/WALLIS, John 10; Jno: 11,
  12; Willm: 10, 11[2]
WALLER, Benja: 35; Mr. Robt: 2,
  15,29
WARD, Eliz: 21; Josha: 25; Patience
  26,27; Thos: 8; Willm: 7
WARENTON, Grace 37; John 37;
  Joseph 37
WARREN/WARRIN, John 4; Jno: 2
WATKINS, Tho: 1,5
WATSON, Abigail 20
WEBB, Mr. Jas: 12[2],14,17,19,20[2],
  21[2],22,23,27[2],28[2],29-31,33,34[2]
WELCH, Sarah 18
WEST, Eliza: 20,21
WESTON, Joseph 18
WHIDON, Capt. John 37; Mrs. John 37
WHITE, Mary 15
WHITEHURST, Bridget,Dorcas,Richart 37
WHITHURST, Elizth:,Sarah, Thos: 37
WHITWELL, Capt. Geo: 8; Mary 8
WILDER, Ann 38; Eliz: 38; house of
  3; Jacob 33,37; Jams: 38; Jno:
  8,18; Jonathan 37; Mary 7; Sarah 37
WILKINS, Lemll: 37[2]; Samuel 12;
  Sarah 37; Willis 12[2]

www.ingramcontent.com/pod-product-compliance
Lightning Source LLC
Chambersburg PA
CBHW081204270326
41930CB00014B/3291